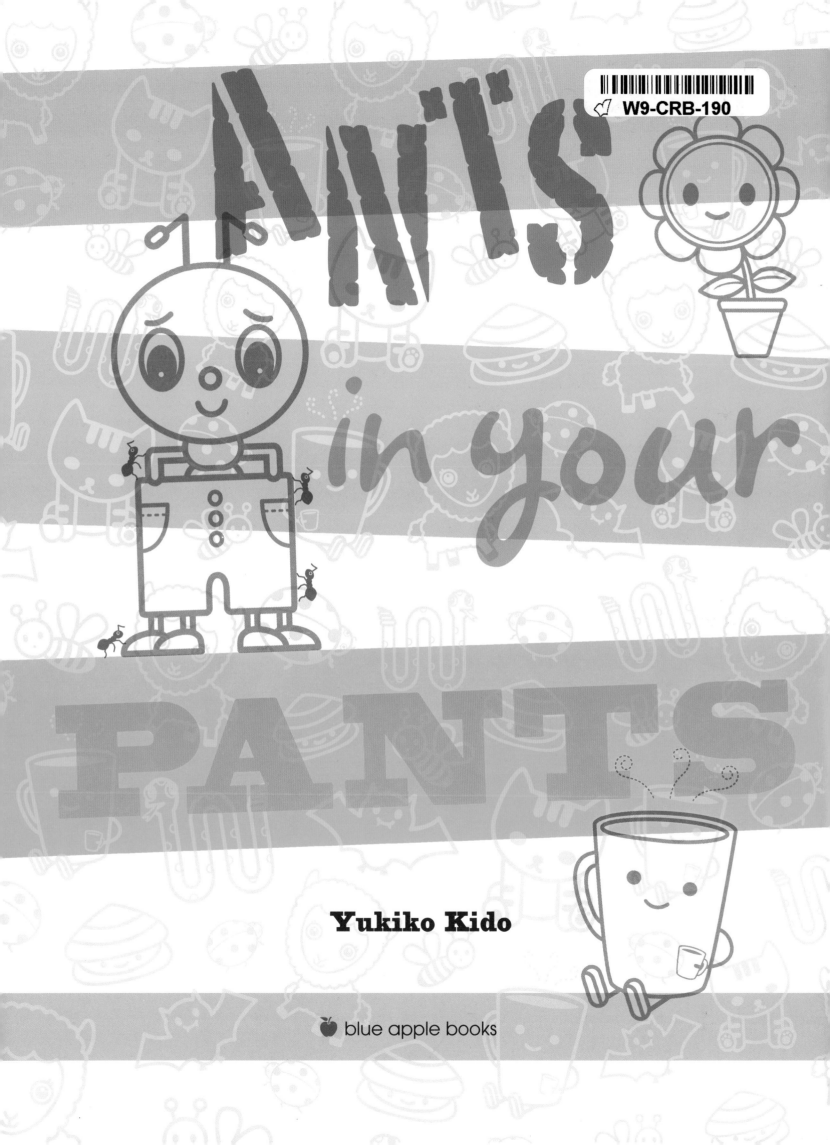

ANTS in your PANTS

Yukiko Kido

blue apple books

pig

p _ _ g

pig in a wig

___ig in a ___ig

dig

d___ ___

pig digs in a wig

___ig ___igs in a ___ig

jig

j___ ___

p_ _ _

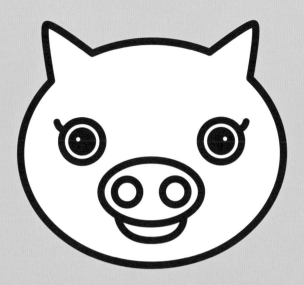

_ _ig

d_ _ _

_ _ig

w_ _ _

_ _ig

Draw a wig for me!

j_ _ _

_ _ig

Put a wig on a pig.

hug

h__g

hug on a rug

___ug on a ___ug

bug

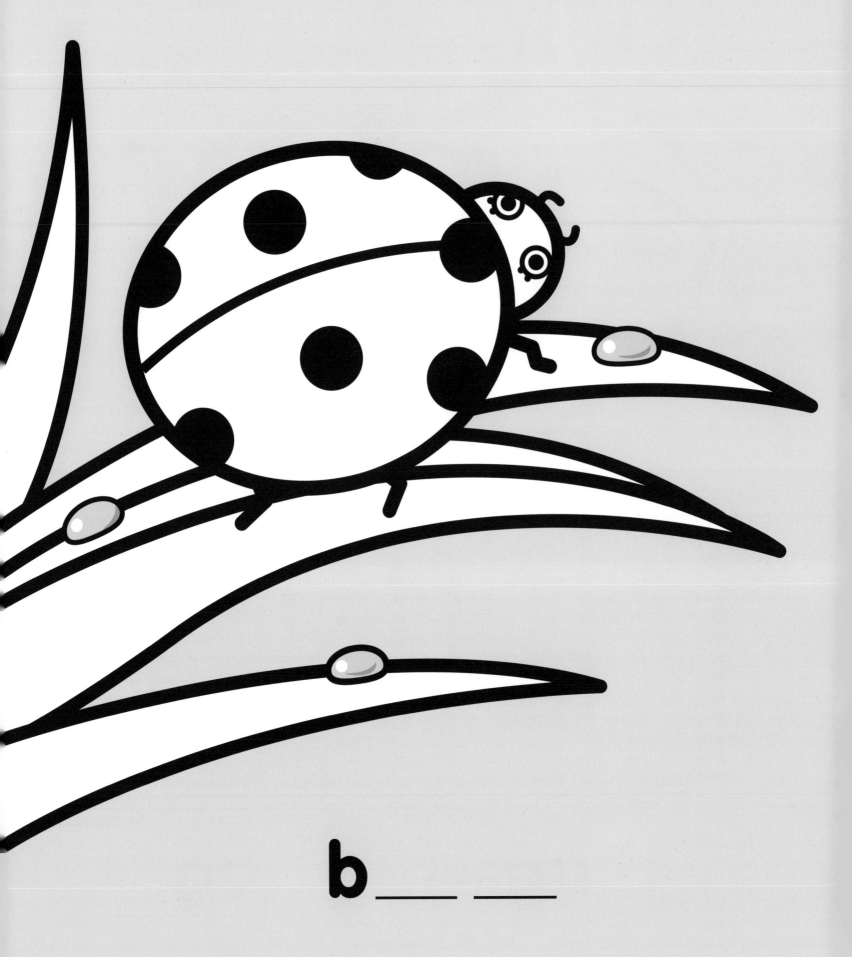

b_____ _____

bugs on a rug

Can you draw a rug?

___ugs on a ___ug

mug

m __ __

bugs and mugs on a rug

Draw bugs!
Draw a mug!

__ugs and __ugs on a __ug

Draw a big bug!

bat

b_a_t_

bat on a rat

Draw a bat on me!

___ at on a ___at

hat

h __ __

___ at

___ ___ ___

___ at

___ ___ ___

___ at

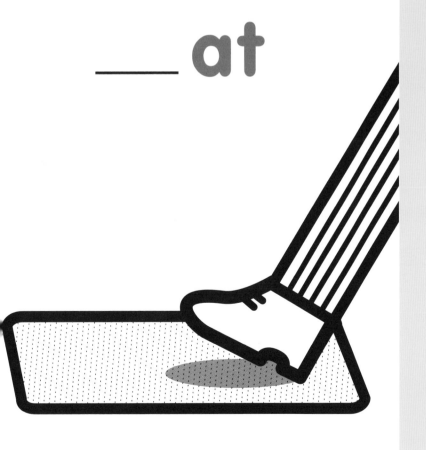

___ ___ ___

___ at

___ ___ ___

Draw a cat on a rug.

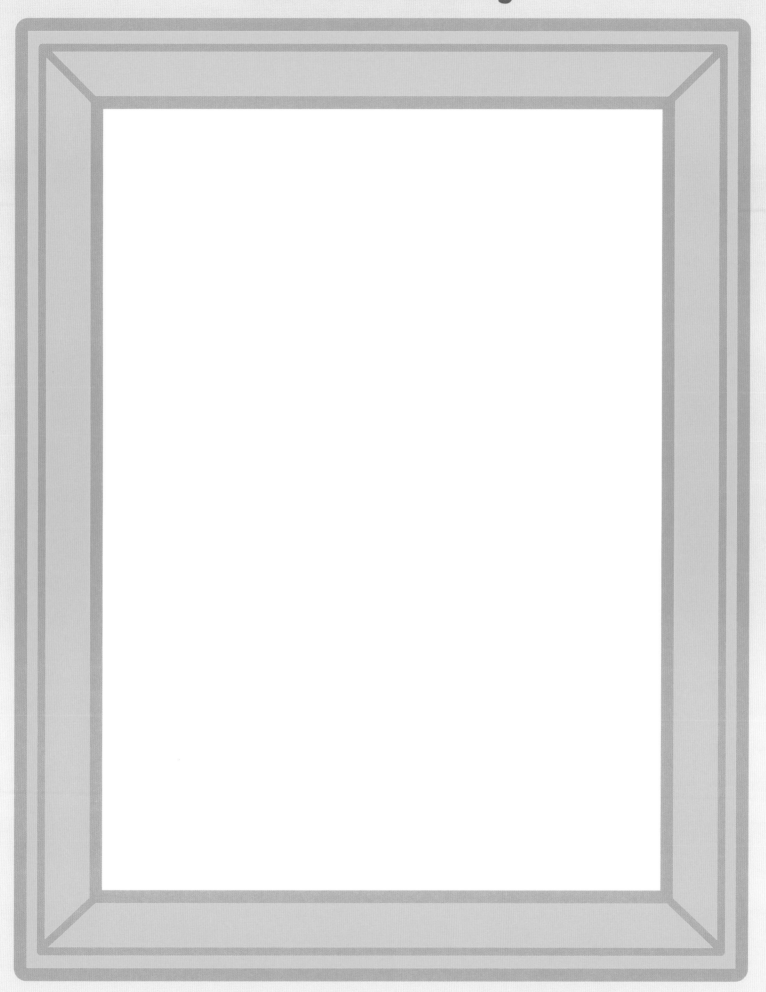

cake

Can you decorate a cake?

c _a_ _k_ _e_

cake bakes

Draw a cake to bake!

__ake __akes

snake

s _ _ _ _ _

snake on a rake

___ __ __ake on a __ __ake

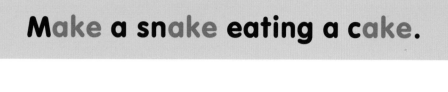

Make a snake eating a cake.

skate

sk_a_t_e__

skate through a gate

_____ate through a __ate

plate

What is your favorite lunch?

pl__ __ __

cake on a plate

___ake on a ___ ___ate

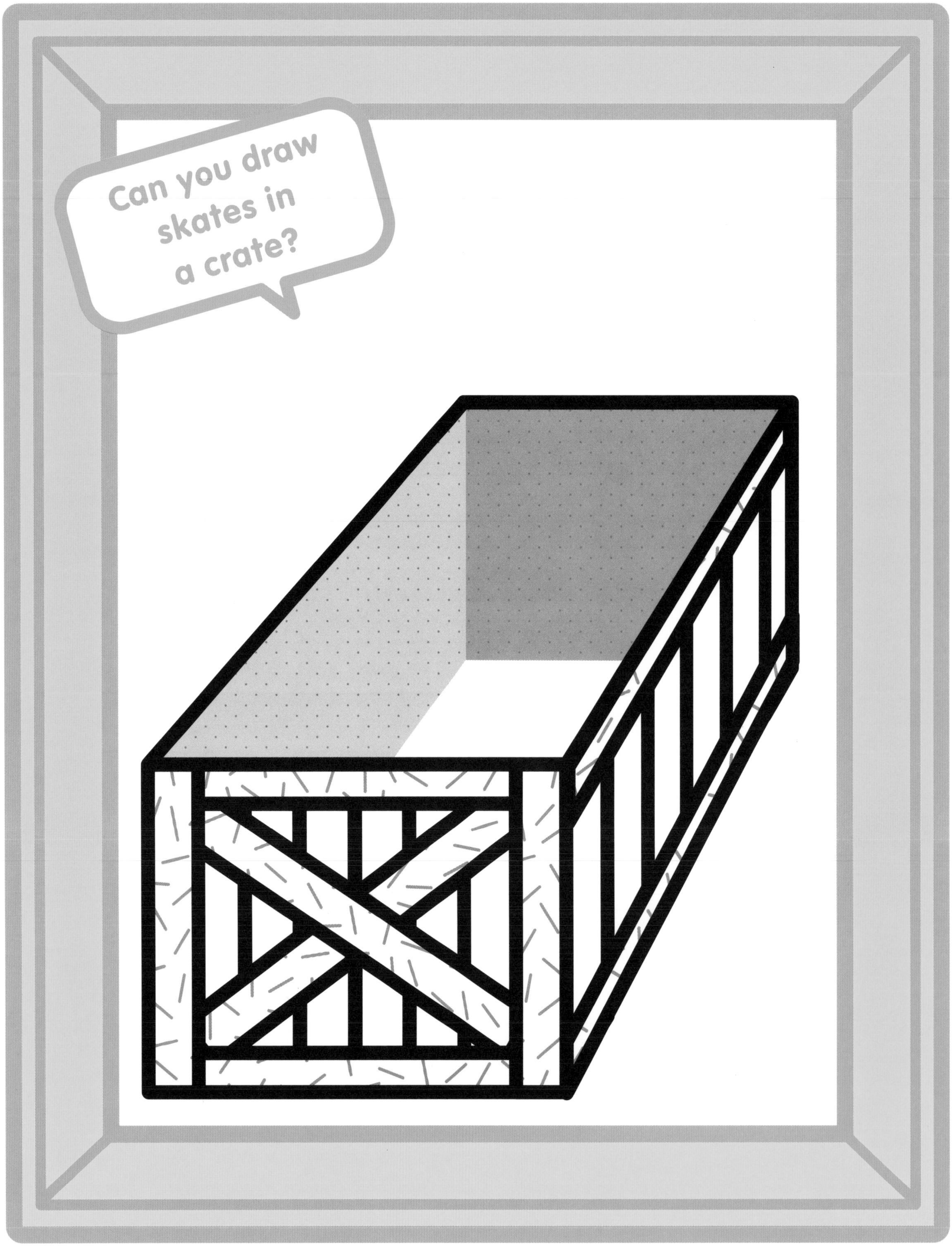
Can you draw skates in a crate?

Draw a pig with a plate.

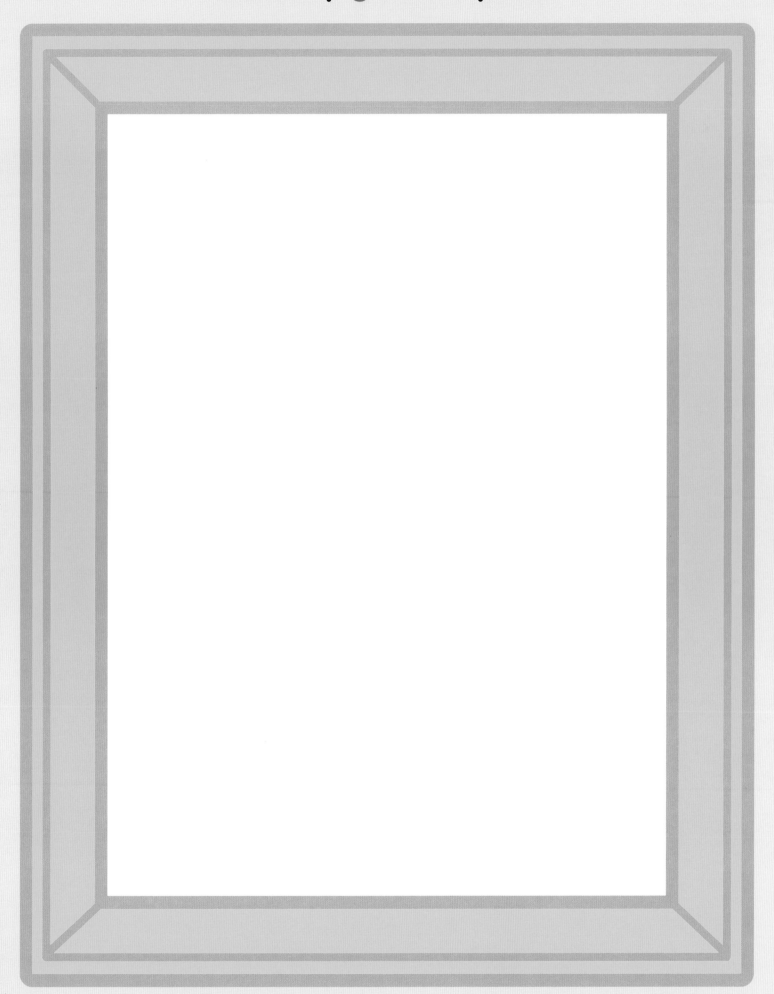

pets

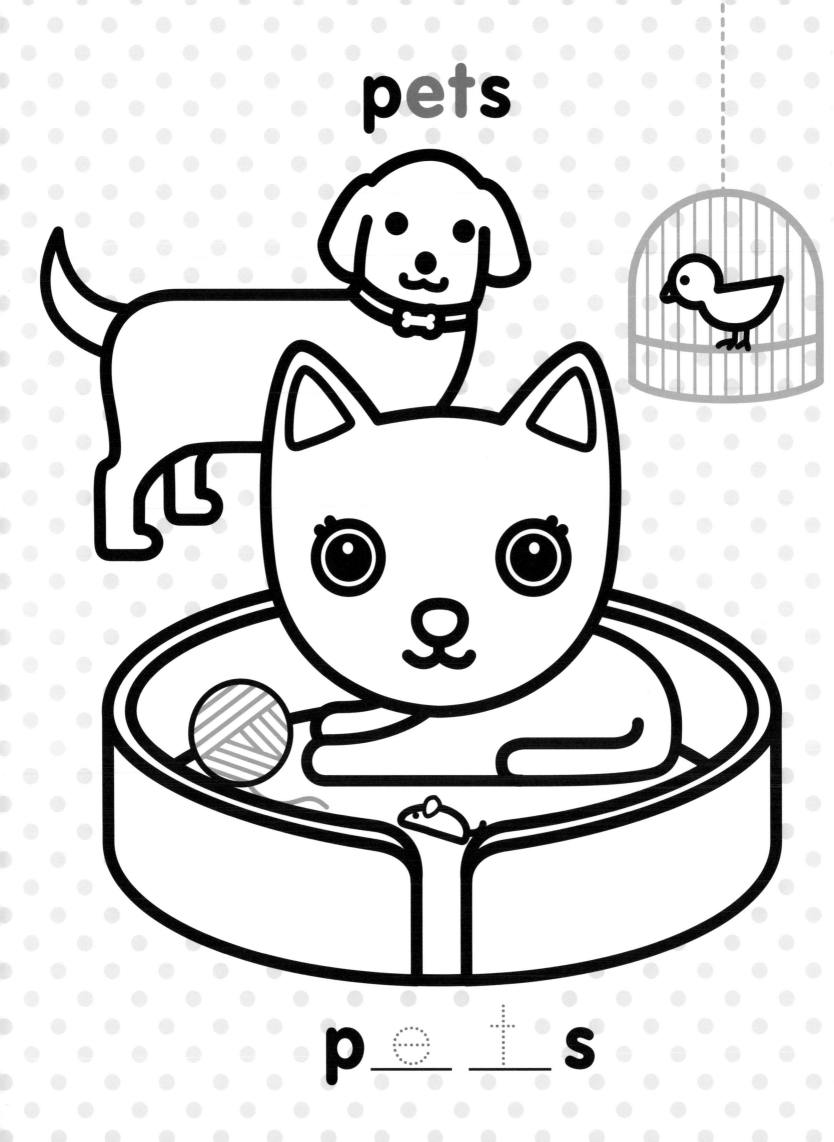

p__e__t__ s

pet net

__ et   __ et

wet pet

__et __et

wet jet

___et ___et

net

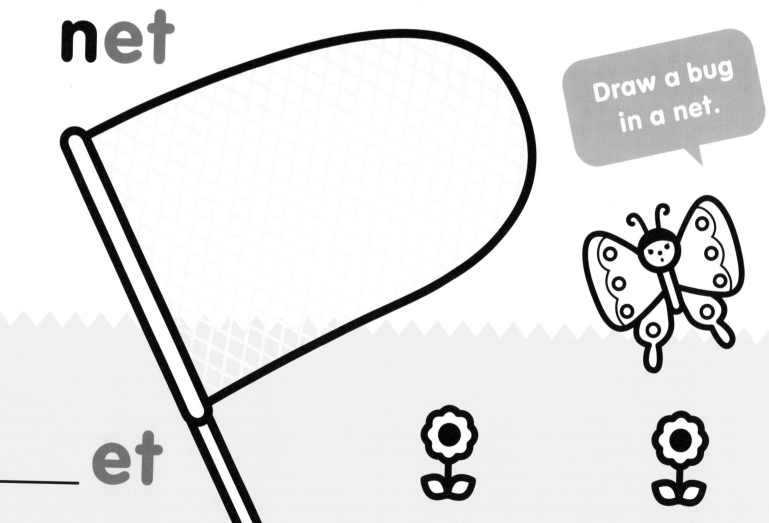

Draw a bug in a net.

___et

float

fl _o_ _a_ _t_

boat floats

___ oat ___ ___ oats

goat on a boat

g_____ on a b_____

goat in a coat

Bye, Bye!

___oat in a___ oat

Draw a coat for me!

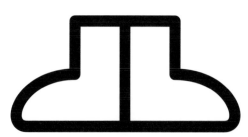

Draw a bat and a bug on a boat.

ant

a n t

ant in pants

ant in ___ants

plants

Draw some more plants!

pl _ _ _ _ s

Draw some bugs on plants!

Draw a goat in pants.

pop

p_o_p

pop on top

___ op on ___ ___ op

cop

c_____ _____

___ ___ op

_ _ _ _

___ op

_ _ _ _

_ op

_ _ _

___ ___ op

_ _ _

Draw three animals who hop on the top!

snow

sn_o_ w_

thr**ow** sn**ow**

___ ___ ___**ow** ___ ___ ___**ow**

bow

b____ ____

__ __ **ow**

__ __ __ **ow**

__ __ **ow**

__ __ __ **ow**

Draw a snow hat.

lamb

l __ __ b

ram

__ am

jam

What is your favorite jam?

j_____ _____

lamb and ram eat jam

__amb and __am eat __am

Draw a ram and goat on a boat.

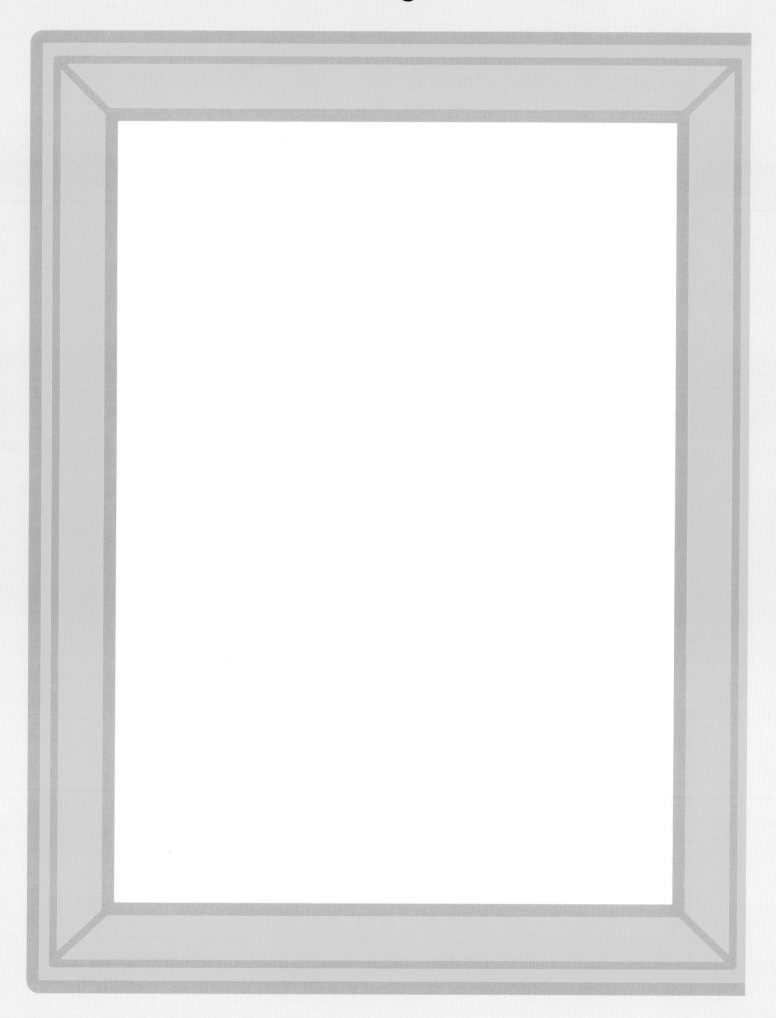

Word-family fun!

ig

Pretty Pig needs a wig! What **"ig"** words can you write?

pig

ug

This mug wants a hug.
What **"ug"** words
can you write?

mug

at

Mr. Bat has no hat!
What **"at"** words
can you write?

bat

ake

ate

Jake the snake likes cake! What **"ake"** words can you write?

Kate loves to skate! What **"ate"** words can you write?

snake	skate

et

Kitty is a wet pet! What "**et**" words can you write?

pet

oat

Little goat is warm in her coat. What "**oat**" words can you write?

goat

ant

A small ant needs bigger pants. What "**ant**" words can you write?

ant

op

This cop wants you to stop! What "**op**" words can you write?

cop

ow ⭐

Do you like to throw snow? What **"ow"** words can you write?

snow

am ⭐

Sam is a happy clam. What **"am"** words can you write?

clam

FUN with Flip-a-Word!

"Children will be instantly attracted to the bold, colorful pictures in these books.... These titles could be used with beginning readers or as an introduction to rhyming words.... appealing cartoon covers and die-cut pages . . ."

—*School Library Journal*

Available Now!

Yukiko Kido

with **220** STICKERS

faces faces everywhere

COLOR + Draw ACTIVITY BOOK

Make a face on a teacup . . .
on a sandwich . . .
or even on a helicopter!